This
Nature Storybook
belongs to:

_____

_____

_____

WALKER BOOKS

Gloucester Old Spot

Tamworth

Large Black

Large White

Saddleback

British Lop

Berkshire

Middle White

Tamworth

Saddleback

Large White

Gloucester Old Spot

Middle White

Large Black

Tamworth

Gloucester Old Spot

Of the pigs
shown on these pages,
the Large White is the one
you're most likely to see
when you visit a farm.
All the other breeds
are rare and need
to be protected.

British Lop

Berkshire

Large White

Saddleback

British Lop

Gloucester Old Spot

First published 1993 by Walker Books Ltd
87 Vauxhall Walk, London SE11 5HJ

This edition published 2008

4 6 8 10 9 7 5 3

Text © 1993 Foxbusters Ltd
Illustrations © 1993 Anita Jeram

Printed in China

British Library Cataloguing in Publication Data:
a catalogue record for this book is available from the British Library

ISBN: 978-1-4063-1196-9

www.walker.co.uk

All Pigs Are Beautiful

Dick King-Smith

illustrated by Anita Jeram

WALKER BOOKS
AND SUBSIDIARIES

LONDON • BOSTON • SYDNEY • AUCKLAND

I love pigs.

I don't care if they're little pigs or big pigs, with long snouts or short snouts, with ears that stick up or ears that flop down. I don't mind if they're black or white or ginger or spotty.

I just love pigs.

If you really twisted my arm and said, "You must have a favourite sort of pig. What is it?" then I might have to say, "A white, black-spotted, middling-snouted, flop-eared pig that comes from Gloucestershire" – though of all the pigs I ever owned, my one particular favourite was a boar called Monty, who was a Large White.

A male breeding pig is called a boar.

The luckiest pigs, like Monty, live outside.

Monty never looked very white,
because he lived out in a wood
where there was a pond in which
he liked to wallow – but he looked
very large. And he was.

A good coating of mud protects a pig from sunburn.

I bought him as a youngster,

  but when he was full-grown he weighed

    six hundred pounds. Monty was so gentle.

When I went out to feed him and his ten wives,

  he would come galloping through the trees to my

    call, a really monstrous and frightening sight

      to anyone who didn't know what

        a soppy old thing he was.

What he really loved, once he'd finished his grub, was to be scratched on the top of his head, between his great ears, and it always affected him in the same way.

A pig can eat everything you can, and more besides. You couldn't digest grass and roots and tubers, for instance ~ but a pig can.

His eyes, with their long pale lashes, would close in ecstasy and slowly his hindquarters would sink down until he was sitting on his bottom like a huge dog. Oh, this is lovely, you could *hear* him thinking. What more can life offer?

Most pigs aren't so fussy. Just having their backs scratched is enough for them – they squirm with pleasure. And of course you must talk to them.

Pigs, like people, enjoy a good chat, so don't just stand there saying nothing.

"Piggy-piggy-piggy" will do if

you don't happen to know the pig's name.

Pigs have a very keen sense of smell. They can smell food even when it's buried underground.

If I'm talking to a big fat sow and don't know what she's called, I usually call her "Mother" or "Mummy". They like that.

A female breeding pig is called a sow.

Sows who live out of doors build large nests of grass, sticks and bracken to have their babies in.

A sow normally has between eight and twelve piglets at a time. Each piglet chooses its own private teat and returns to it for every feed.

Sows spend their lives having babies,
loads of them, and they take as good
care of them as your mum does of you. Well, almost.
Trouble is, newborn piglets are so small that
sometimes the sow lies down and squashes one.
Your mother would never do that
to you – I hope!

Of course, while you're busy talking to pigs, telling
them how lovely they are or their babies are,
the pigs are talking back.

Those who don't know much about them just hear grunts and squeaks, but there are all sorts of things a pig might be saying to you, if you understood the language, such as:

Young female pigs are called gilts.

As you can see, pigs have cloven hoofs. They walk on their third and fourth toes.

Once a sow has been mated, the farmer expects her piglets to be born three months, three weeks and three days later.

"How kind of you to admire my children," or

"Scratch a little harder, please – up a bit, a little bit to the left, down a bit, yes, that's it!" or

"Well, yes, actually you're not the first person to call me beautiful," or

"This food is really excellent, yum, yum, thanks a bunch."

But of course, pigs, like people,

aren't always sunny and good-tempered,

and you might hear:

"Hurry up, you stupid

two-legged creature,

I'm starving hungry and you're late!" or

"Don't you dare pick up
one of my babies or
I'll bite you!"
(And you be careful
– pigs have a horrible bite
so don't take liberties.)

Pigs know their own minds, like people,

which makes them difficult to drive.

Pigs that are well kept and well fed rarely need the vet.

A pig's insides are pretty well exactly the same as ours, too. Heart and lungs and liver and kidneys and stomach – they're all in the same places as ours are, and pigs, like people, can eat meat or vegetables or both.

Like people (or at any rate people once they've been potty-trained), pigs are very clean in their habits and will never foul their own nests.

Have you noticed how often

I've said that pigs are like people?

That's one of the reasons I like them so much.

There's one big difference, though.

People can be good-looking or
just ordinary-looking or plain ugly.
But all pigs are beautiful.

Gloucester Old Spot

Large Black

Large White

British Lop

Look up the pages to find out about
all these piggy things. Don't forget
to look at both kinds of words:
this kind and **this kind**.

Berkshire

Tamworth

Saddleback

Large White

Gloucester Old Spot

Middle White

Large Black

Tamworth

Gloucester Old Spot

Saddleback

Berkshire

Tamworth

Saddleback

British Lop

Gloucester Old Spot

A note from the author

Dick King-Smith says, "I wrote *All Pigs are Beautiful* in memory of my favourite pig, a large white boar called Monty. The title is not a joke – I mean it."

A note from the illustrator

Anita Jeram lived near a farm that kept pigs when she was illustrating this book. "I visited them there," she says, "sketched them, scratched them behind their ears, and generally got to know them. They were all beautiful, and I began to wish I had a pig of my own."

Which of these Nature Storybooks have you read?

Growing Frogs
ISBN 978-1-4063-1206-5

All Pigs Are Beautiful
ISBN 978-1-4063-1196-9

One Tiny Turtle
ISBN 978-1-4063-1198-3

Think of an Eel
ISBN 978-1-4063-1201-0

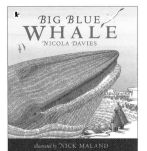

Big Blue Whale
ISBN 978-1-4063-1257-7

Caterpillar Butterfly
ISBN 978-1-4063-1277-5

A Field Full of Horses
ISBN 978-1-4063-1280-5

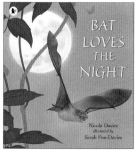

Bat Loves the Night
ISBN 978-1-4063-1275-1

T. Rex
ISBN 978-1-4063-1290-4

Surprising Sharks
ISBN 978-1-4063-1287-4

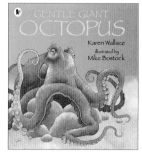

Gentle Giant Octopus
ISBN 978-1-4063-1284-3

Tigress
ISBN 978-1-4063-1296-6

Ice Bear
ISBN 978-1-4063-1304-8

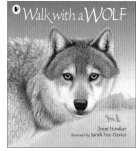

Walk with a Wolf
ISBN 978-1-4063-1308-6

White Owl, Barn Owl
ISBN 978-1-4063-1312-3

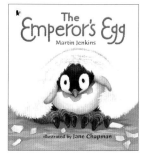

The Emperor's Egg
ISBN 978-1-4063-1301-7

Tracks of a Panda
ISBN 978-1-4063-1871-5

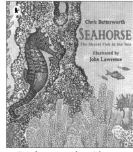

**Seahorse: the Shyest
Fish in the Sea**
ISBN 978-1-4063-2010-7

I Love Guinea-pigs
ISBN 978-1-4063-1872-2

Bears in the Forest
ISBN 978-1-4063-1870-8